BUDGETING: FUNDAMENTAL GUIDE FOR BEGINNERS

A SIMPLE PRACTICAL APPROACH TO MANGAGING YOUR EVERYDAY FINANCES & SAVING FOR THE FUTURE

BY CRAIG SANTORO

Published by

ALEX-PUBLISHING

"Many people take no care of their money till they come nearly to the end of it, and others do just the same with their time."

– Johann Wolfgang von Goethe

Author's Note:

Somebody once said that failing to plan is planning to fail. And failing to manage is managing to fail. Just like an untended garden, many important areas of our lives can be very messy to say the least without good active management. One of those areas is personal finance.

Meeting responsibilities on a daily basis while also trying to save for your future can seem impossible. Sometimes just meeting your minimum financial obligations can be a nightmare. There are things you can do to make it manageable.

The biggest problem that most people face is that they simply don't know how to budget. You may try to set money aside for bills and other expenses. You may watch your bank balances closely to make sure you don't overdraft. Often this is not enough. Planning is necessary.

Today budgeting is taught in high school. Most schools offer a financial management class that is required for graduation. This means that the most recent generations will be armed with the knowledge they need to manage their finances. For those who are older, budgeting is not something that was taught. It was something you learned by trial and error, if at all. This lack of education and skills has led to a staggering number of Americans living from paycheck to paycheck, with no idea how to bring themselves out of the rut.

This book is aimed toward those who do not have experience or knowledge of budgeting. It will take you through three methods of budgeting, and the steps necessary to make them work. By the end of this book you should be prepared to begin budgeting and achieve a long awaited financial stability.

Thanks,

Craig Santoro

TABLE OF CONTENT

Living Paycheck to Paycheck

Are you tired of the constant feeling that you don't have any money? Living paycheck to paycheck is a real problem for many people. While some of the people in this rut are low earning families, many are not. Those in the middle class can also become entrenched in this cycle.

There is an old saying that you will spend what you earn. Generally it is expected that you are living within your means and meeting all of your financial obligations. At the same time, you don't have any money left over. As you earn more money you take on additional expenses or luxuries that eat up the additional income. This is how many families fall into the paycheck to paycheck cycle.

It is very possible to break this cycle. You have to have some willpower. You have to force yourself to deal with delayed gratification. Here are some tips for breaking the cycle.

The Importance of Curbing Spending

Most people who have trouble making ends meet or running out of money before the next paycheck hits actually spend quite a bit on unnecessary expenses. When you cut back on some of the luxuries of life you will find that you can save vast amounts of money. Even if it is something as simple as choosing an off brand at the grocery store, all of those pennies and dollars add up quickly. Here are a few ways you can curb your spending.

1. Limit fast food trips to two per month
2. Buy off brands at the grocery store
3. Shop thrift stores for clothing before going to department stores
4. Limit entertainment such as movies and concerts to one per month
5. Cut out or cut down your cable or satellite bill
6. Cut back on cell phone usage and bills
7. Never use payday loans—they cost more than they're worth
8. Cut back on driving to the bare minimum to save on gas
9. Turn up the thermostat in the summer and down in the winter—dress for the weather instead of compensating with high energy bills
10. Cut out or cut back on vices such as soda and cigarettes
11. Make your own desserts instead of buying prepackaged cookies and cakes

These are just some of the ways you can trim the fat from your spending. Carefully consider where you spend money that you don't need to spend. Anything you can cut back would be beneficial. At the same time, don't deny yourself every pleasure. You have to feel like you are benefiting from your frugal lifestyle and all of your hard work. Denying yourself every luxury all the time will cause you to give up on budgeting.

The Importance of Saving for the Future

One of the biggest problems with living paycheck to paycheck is that you don't save back any money for the future. Whether you are looking five years ahead or thirty, it is important to save at least a small amount from each paycheck toward your long term goals.

Of course, the big savings goal many people think about is their retirement. If you are younger than 40, this event may seem so far in the future that it is hardly worth worrying about. However, this is the attitude that is leaving many middle aged adults struggling to figure out what they are going to do when they have to retire. Saving money for your retirement needs to start at a younger age. If you start early, you can save a large amount of money without hurting your average income and spending.

There are many other things that are closer to the present that you might want to save up for. If you are close to any of these events, or you just want to be prepared for them in the future, you should definitely start saving now. Here are just a few.

- A wedding for yourself or your child
- Preparing for a baby
- College tuition for a child
- A car that you don't have to make payments on
- A down payment on a house that will save you on housing costs
- A nest egg for maintenance or replacement of major appliances as they age
- A family vacation that your children will remember for a lifetime

Saving money isn't just about surviving. It's about living. Without saving back money for the little things, and the big things, that come along in life, you will fail to truly enjoy them when they arrive because you will be struggling to pay for them. Planning ahead not only keeps you prepared for emergencies, but also decreases stress and increases overall happiness.

How Budgeting Helps You Meet Your Goals

Budgeting is an important step in helping you meet your goals. Budgeting isn't just about being careful with your money. You can use budgeting tools to help you plan your income and spending so that you can intentionally set aside savings. You can use expense tracking to help you trim the fat from your budget and see where you can make changes to improve your overall quality of life, now and in the future. Your long term financial goals, as well as your short term way of life, can only be realized through effective budgeting.

Methods of Budgeting

There are three primary ways to budget. You can budget by week or pay period, month, or by expense. Budgeting by expense is the easiest way to budget. It is generally done by using the envelope method, which will be explained shortly. Budgeting by week or pay period can help you stop the paycheck to paycheck cycle, but works with that mentality while you work to improve your financial habits. Monthly budgeting is helpful because you can see everything you spend monthly at one time. This is important because many bills are only paid once per month.

You may choose to use a combination of methods. Sometimes it can be helpful to have even the most basic monthly budget to use in combination with a weekly budget. It can also help to use the envelope method, especially if you have difficulty setting aside money for larger expenses.

Budgeting Basics

Regardless of what method you use to budget, you will need to understand some basic concepts that must be used. These tools and concepts are vitally important to your budgeting success. They should be used diligently, especially when you are just starting out. You will need to use the information from these tools to help you create effective and accurate budgets.

Tracking Income

There are some important things to keep in mind when tracking income. You want your budget to be as accurate as possible. If you overestimate how much income you will have you could throw your entire budget off balance. You could wind up short for the week or month, and be unable to pay an important bill.

When you consider your income for your budget you should calculate all *reliable* sources of income. This means that you need to incorporate only that income which is guaranteed. This is usually your paycheck. When you calculate the money you will have, don't use your gross pay. If you work the same number of hours per week you can use the net pay from your check stubs to see what you can budget for income. If your work hours vary, calculate your gross income and deduct 25% for taxes. You may have fewer deductions than that, but it is better to be safe than sorry.

You may have other sources of income such as that from a side job, child support or alimony. If you have steady income from one or more of these sources that is guaranteed, feel free to add it to your budgeted income. Guaranteed income is income that is received on a scheduled basis. It also must be received with continuity, such as on time each period for at least three to six months.

If you have a child support or alimony order but the money doesn't always come on time or at all, you should not count it as income in your budget. If you budget for this income and then it doesn't show up it will throw your entire financial plan out of whack and you will have to face potentially serious consequences.

Tracking Expenses

There are many ways that you can track your expenses and spending. Tracking expenses is especially important when you first start budgeting. It is vital that you know where all of your money is going. Creating a budget of what you anticipate spending is an important aspect of your budget. But tracking expenses tells you where your money is actually going.

Tracking expenses is important because it helps you determine what you need to budget for. Bills like rent and a car payment are fixed expenses that you don't really have to think about. But most expenses are variable, meaning that they are different each month. The only way to budget for variable expenses is to have some idea of what that amount might be.

It is pretty easy to track your expenses. You can easily create a spreadsheet on your computer where you can enter your expenses daily and have a monthly total running at the bottom. There are such spreadsheets available online as well. This requires keeping receipts and entering each expense.

You can also get expense trackers on your smart phone with many different available apps. This is helpful for making sure that you don't miss any expenses when you enter them into your tracking at home. If you are single you can just use the expense tracker app. If you have a significant other you will need to combine your tracking and theirs on a master spreadsheet or software.

Budgeting for Variable Expenses

This is where your expense tracker will come in handy. When you track your spending for the previous month you can use that information to help you budget for your variable expenses for the following month. As you continue this trend you can calculate the average spending for that item based on several months of data. This will give you the most accurate budget possible.

It is important that you give yourself some leeway when it comes to variable expenses. You should always pad them, even if just by a few dollars, when doing your budget. This way you will not run into serious problems if the expense ends up being a bit more than you thought. If you have extra money at the end of the budget period because you padded your variable expenses you can use that money to help make larger purchases that you couldn't afford before, or you can add it to your savings nest egg.

It is best to budget as closely as possible. As already mentioned your expense tracker can help you with some of that. Past spending habits can help you calculate the budget for things like gasoline, food and household items. Some variable expenses require a different tactic.

For utility bills, for example, you will want to look back at your previous bills for the current season. In other words, if it is summer you need to look back to see what the average bill was in the previous summer. This can usually be done by contacting your utility company and requesting the information. If this is your first season in your home you can still contact the utility company and they will give you average utility costs for that month in the previous year based on the previous resident's usage.

Grocery Budget Tips

Budgeting for groceries is perhaps one of the most difficult variable expenses to calculate. Food prices vary greatly. Sometimes you can get great deals and catch awesome sales, and sometimes you will have to pay full price no matter where in the city you go to shop. Meat prices rise and fall. Any number of things can change the price of food with little or no notice.

Your previous spending will give you a starting point for your grocery budget. Look back through several months of spending to get an idea of the average amount you spend. Try to go with the higher number just to make sure that you have enough budgeted.

It also helps to make a meal plan for the budget period, make a grocery list, and estimate the amount of money you will spend to fulfill that list. Again, pad the budget a bit to make sure you have enough money for groceries in case prices rise or something unexpected comes up.

There is one great tool that you can use to help you make your grocery budget more accurate. You can build a spreadsheet for it. There are also a few apps and websites that will help you do this. You have to track every item that you buy. You bring home your grocery receipt and input the store, date, item, size, and price. By doing this you will be able to see exactly what you pay for each item.

When you create a meal plan for the next budget period you can look back at your itemized list and see what you paid for each item. Your grocery list will be made and you will have an almost exact dollar amount of what you will spend. Not everyone has the time to do this, but if you can it is a great tool that can really help you.

The Envelope Method

The envelope method is the simplest way to budget. This is the method that has been taught to young people for years before budgeting software and apps were commonplace. All you need are some regular mailing envelopes and somewhere safe to keep them.

Why It Works

The envelope method works well for people who need to visually see what they need to pay and where their money is going. It is also a great way to budget if you aren't good with computers or number crunching. Budgeting using envelopes also works extremely well for people who pay using cash.

If you don't have a checking account or prefer to work with cash then envelope budgeting is extremely helpful. It allows you to set aside money so that it isn't just sitting in your wallet. This way you don't spend money that you need for a particular expense.

The Process

To use the envelope method you will need to have some mailing envelopes and a safe place to store them. A fire safe is fairly inexpensive. You can get a small one for around $50. Not only will having your money stored out of sight help you keep from spending it, it will also help keep it from being stolen.

You will need to first determine your most basic expenses that you need to budget for. Make a list of every type of expense you will have throughout the month. You will then create an envelope for each expense on your list. Here is an example list:

- Rent
- Electric bill
- Gas bill
- Water bill
- Phone bill
- Car payment
- Gasoline
- Groceries
- Household items
- Dining and Entertainment

If you don't have a savings account you may also want to make a list of savings goals. You would then have an envelope for each of those as well. These are usually short term savings goals such as:

- Buying new tires for your car
- Buying a computer, television or other big ticket item
- Buying needed furniture or beds
- Buying needed clothing
- Saving for an anticipated move

- Fund for unexpected car maintenance
- Fun for other unexpected expenses

On each envelope write the name of the expense and the amount you need to put into the envelope each month. For savings envelopes write the total amount you want to save for that item. Number your savings envelopes in order of priority.

When you get money you will divide it into your necessary envelopes. Start with the most important expenses such as rent, utilities and groceries. If you drive your car payment and gasoline will need to come next. Save non-essential expenses for last. Once all of your expense envelopes have the correct amount in them you can begin dividing the rest into your savings envelopes.

It is likely that you get paid more than once per month, but most of your bills will be paid only once per month. It is best if you pay all of your bills at the first of the month. In order to do this you will need to put some money aside each paycheck to each monthly bill. Then at the beginning of the month you will have the money you need to pay each of your bills. Examples of monthly bills are rent and utilities.

Your variable expenses that occur throughout the month on an almost daily basis will be handled a bit differently. After you have put money aside in the monthly bill envelopes you will place money into your variable expense envelopes. Make sure that you have the minimum amount for your pay period in the envelopes. For example, you may have budgeted $400 for groceries for the month. If you get paid weekly you would put $100 per week into the envelope.

As you proceed through the month, use the money in each envelope only for that expense to which it is dedicated. If you really want to go out to eat but your dining envelope is empty, don't take money out of the grocery envelope to satisfy your craving. It is important that you only use the money for what it has been set aside.

Gauging Success
The envelope method doesn't really use precise expense tracking. You don't record each purchase or figure out exactly what you spent the money on. Instead, your success is gauged by what is left in your envelopes and if you have met all of your responsibilities for the month.

If your savings envelopes are gradually increasing then you know you are doing a great job. The more money you are able to save the more clear it is that you are staying within your budget.

There are also signs that you are not succeeding. For example, you could run out of money in your grocery envelope before your next paycheck. When this happens it could pay to track your spending in that area a bit more closely to make sure you aren't overspending. Maybe you should buy more veggies and fewer meats to save money.

Budgeting by Payday

Budgeting by payday is one of the most common ways to budget. After all, it is easier to see where your money is going and needs to go when you look at it from when you get the money. There are benefits and drawbacks to budgeting by payday. If you are used to living from paycheck to paycheck it is easier to wrap your head around. However, if you have long term goals or a lot of monthly bills it might not make sense to use this method.

Why It Works

Budgeting by payday works well because you can plan how your money will be spent as it comes in. If you are trying to look at the big picture you can lose sight of how the money you currently have needs to be spent. Budgeting by payday helps you see exactly where your money needs to go right now.

Budgeting by payday works even when you have regular monthly bills. You can save a portion of the monthly bill, such as rent, from each payday and pay it when it is due. This way you can maintain your regular bills without worrying about where the money will come from.

If you need help figuring out how to break up your paycheck and how to spend it wisely, budgeting by payday can really benefit you. The key to success is to maintain savings for the bigger items and monthly payments that you have to take care of. If you fail to plan for these things in your weekly or biweekly budget you will find yourself hurting financially very quickly.

The Process

The first thing you need to do is determine what your monthly bills are. Make a list of each bill that must be paid monthly, variable or fixed. This usually includes things like rent, utilities and car payments. Divide each bill by the number of paydays you have in one month. This is the amount you will need to set aside each payday for that bill. These are fixed amounts that you will record as expenses every payday based budget.

The second thing you need to do is determine what daily expenses you have that need to be covered every payday. These will be things like food and gasoline. Anything that you pay every single payday should be listed here, along with estimated amounts of what you will spend on that item. Use the expense tracking mentioned in chapter one to help you determine what amount you should budget.

Once you have a list of all of your expenses you can look at your income. Your paycheck is likely about the same every payday. Take this average income amount and subtract all of your pay period expenses from it. This will give you a remainder of what you can save for long term goals or upcoming larger expenditures. If your total expenses is more than your income for that period you will need to review your budget and see where you can cut corners.

Once you have worked out the kinks you will have a payday budget that you can use every single pay period. You won't have to rework the budget unless your income or one of your expenses changes. Every pay period should be about the same. Eventually this will lead to basic spending habits and you won't have to refer to your written budget hardly at all.

If you have an expense come up that is not part of your regular budget you will need to alter your budget for that payday. If it is a large expenditure you may have to dip into savings. If you have some warning that the expense is coming up you can budget for it the same way you do your monthly bills. Just set aside a small amount each payday so that you have the total amount when you need it.

When Income Varies

If you have a highly variable income you will need to take a different approach. When your income varies greatly a pay period budget is a great way to go. It will help you make sure that you cover all of the expenses necessary to life before spending any other money.

If you have variable income you will not be able to have a set budget for every pay period. Instead you will need to prepare your budget for that payday as soon as you know how much that check will be. Use the same methods outlined above. Make sure that your most important bills are covered first. Your rent, utilities and groceries should take top priority. Take care of these expenses first, then worry about the rest of your spending for the pay period.

You might not want to break up the monthly bills into equal "payments" over each pay period. If one payday is drastically lower than the other you could wind up not having enough to pay the bill when it is due. Instead set aside as much of your income for that first pay period of the month as you can. You'll likely have the money for that bill long before it is due and have one pay period at the end of the month with a lot of leeway. That is preferable to being caught off guard and not being able to pay your rent.

When You Have Tip Income

Tip income is perhaps the hardest to budget. You never know what tips you are going to get in a shift. Some days are bound to be better than others. Some days you will feel like you are working for free. So how do you budget for this income on a per payday budget?

The best thing to do is to deposit your tips directly into your checking or savings account. Leave the money there and pretend it does not exist until you start your next pay period budget. That way your tip income will be included in your regular payday budget, and you won't have the cash burning a hole in your pocket.

Gauging Success

The first thing you will notice when this budget is working properly is that you never run out of money before the next payday. You will always be able to cover everything you need to, and without being completely broke. Even if you have only a few dollars left when that next check hits, you have accomplished keeping yourself from overspending, and you are likely living within your means. Hopefully you are managing to build up a nest egg as well.

The second thing you will notice when you use this budget wisely is that your monthly bills are paid—and it doesn't seem like a hardship. When you try to pay your rent out of one check you can feel like you don't even have enough money to eat. But when you break up that rent payment over multiple pay periods, you feel like you can breathe. It is much less stressful to budget for bills in this fashion.

Finally, when this budget is being used properly you will discover that you have more money than you thought you did. If you stick to the budget you make you will be able to easily afford everything you need, and perhaps some things that you want.

Budgeting by Month

If you like seeing the big picture you will want to budget by month. Budgeting by month makes sense because most bills are paid on a monthly basis. When you budget by payday you are budgeting for income, but when you are budgeting by month you are budgeting for bills.

Why It Works

Budgeting by month works well for people who have a lot of monthly bills. It is best for people who have more than just rent or utilities to pay each month. People who budget by month probably have credit card payments, loan payments, rent or mortgage payments, car payments and the like. They probably have more luxury bills as well such as cell phone bills and cable or satellite.

When you have a lot of monthly bills it is better to budget by month because you need to see the big picture. It is too difficult to make sure all of your bills are paid by looking at it from a pay period point of view. If you budgeted that many monthly bills by pay period you would be setting aside a dozen small amounts from each paycheck, making your budgeting extremely complicated. The more complicated your budgeting method is, the harder it is to stick to it and be successful.

The Process

In many ways budgeting by month is easier than budgeting by pay period. The first thing you do is calculate your expected income for the month. Include all sources of guaranteed income such as salary and regularly paid child support or alimony. If you have variable income include that as well, but be conservative in your estimates of how much you will earn.

The next thing you need to do is make a list of all of your monthly bills. If you have variable monthly bills such as utilities you should pad these a bit to make sure that you have them covered. It is better to plan to spend more than to not have enough when the time comes to pay your bills.

Then list all of your other expenses such as groceries, household and personal items, and gasoline. You may want to budget luxury expenses as well such as entertainment or dining, vices such as cigarettes, or for gifts.

Make a list of your upcoming large expenditures or things that you are saving for. Decide on an amount you will add to your savings for these things each month. You will want to plan an amount that will be easily met and fit well within your budget without making you strapped.

Add up all of your income and then your expenses. Your expenses should be less than your income. Even if you are just $20 lower than your income, you are doing well. You want to have at least a little bit of leeway in your budget in case something comes up.

This is all there is to your monthly budget. Pretty simple, right? The hard part is making sure you follow your budget.

Gauging Success

It is much harder to stick to a monthly budget. You are probably not being paid monthly. You will have to make sure that you have the money to meet all of your obligations. This means really watching your spending over the course of the month. You will have to split up your bills and pay some out of each pay period. Usually this is determined by when they are due. If you have a lot of bills due at once you will have to split them up so that some are paid early.

If you manage to pay all of your monthly obligations, feed yourself, keep your car running, and have money to set back in savings, you are doing a great job of budgeting for the month. If you find that you are a bit short at the end of the month, you are probably spending too much earlier in the month and will need to reevaluate your spending habits. This may mean budgeting by payday for a couple of months to get used to how to break up your spending and bills.

Budgeting Tools

While it is possible to simply grab paper and pen and make up a budget, it really isn't very efficient. In days gone by people used ledgers to track their income and expenses on ledgers, if at all. Today we have computers. Nearly everyone has a computer, a smart phone, or both. You can use these to your advantage in budgeting.

There are many different tools you can use in your budgeting. Which ones you choose will depend on your level of comfort with computers and various software. You might want to check into all of the options and decide which one works best for you. Some tools are very straightforward and others are more complex.

Spreadsheets

Spreadsheets can be one of your best friends when it comes to budgeting. A spreadsheet is like a fancy ledger. But you can do much more with a spreadsheet than a simple ledger.

Creating a simple payday or monthly budget really doesn't require a spreadsheet. However, it can be handy to use a spreadsheet for these, simply because you can easily put in a formula to do all of the math for you. This helps eliminate math errors that can seriously affect the effectiveness of your budget.

Spreadsheets are most helpful when tracking your income and expenses. You can use a spreadsheet to track every dime that goes in and out of your pocket. This spreadsheet should have one entry per day of the month. It should have a column for every source of income and every expense. For each day you will enter everything you had come in or go out for that day. Simply enter the amount in the appropriate column. At the end of the 31 rows you will have formulas that automatically total the amount that you spent on each category for the month.

You can either create your own spreadsheets or download spreadsheets that have already been created. The Microsoft Office website has hundreds of budgeting templates for Excel. You can find many more budgeting and expense tracking spreadsheets online in numerous sources for nearly any software.

If you decide to use spreadsheets you should have at least a basic knowledge of how to manipulate the spreadsheets. Even if you download one that is already designed you will likely need to alter it to meet your needs. You may not have the same income and expenses as the person that designed the spreadsheet. It is rare to find one that exactly matches what you are looking for. You will probably have to make at least a few changes to make it work for you.

For this reason people who are very proficient with spreadsheets may find it better to create their own. You can create whole budgeting workbooks in Excel, with a sheet for expense tracking, one for budgeting, and one for a summary of how well you are sticking to your budget. You can link them all together in one workbook so that you only have to enter data once. This is a great way to budget, but it takes a very savvy computer user.

Another way you can use spreadsheets is in your grocery budgeting. You can create a spreadsheet that has columns for date purchased, store, brand, item, size and price. By tracking this information you will be able to turn a variable expense into a more easily controlled amount.

Software

There are a lot of different software applications out there for budgeting. Some are free, some you pay for once, and some are subscription based. Some are downloadable to your computer and others are web based. They all have different features and different capabilities.

Choosing a budgeting software can be tricky business. You can easily start using a software and decide within a month that you absolutely hate it. Not every software will work for every household. Different people will expect different features, and some people will need more help with their budgeting than others.

Software or Web Application?

One of the first questions you have to answer is if you want a stand-alone software on your computer or you want to use a web app. There are upsides and downsides to both. You have to decide what is more important to you.

With a web app you can access your budget from anywhere. You won't have to feel tied to your computer. If you need to take a trip and you don't have that computer with you, you will still have access to your budget to make sure you stay on track.

The downside to a web app is security. All web apps are supposed to be secure. They should have a security certificate to prove it. Unfortunately, even the most secure applications can be hacked. This has been proven time and again with scandals such as the stealing of credit card information from Target. If you are worried about your personal information being on the internet, you probably don't want to use a web based app.

With a software application you don't have the portability you do with a web app. However you do have the security of having your personal information stored directly on your computer. Software applications usually have more features as well, such as being able to import your bank information directly into your software to avoid making manual entries for expenses.

Common Features to Consider

There are a lot of different features available depending on what software you choose. Some common features you will find across all software are:

- Input for expected income
- Input for expected expenses in either predetermined categories or categories you create
- Input for actual spending
- Reporting of how your spending relates to your budget

These are the most basic features that are in all software. The most basic software offers nothing else. It will generally only offer the ability to enter expenses and income in predetermined programmed categories, and you won't be able to add your own. This usually applies to free software.

There are some features that are available with more advanced software. Not all of these features will be in every software, but you can take a look at this list to get an idea of what you want to look for in a software.

- The ability to add your own expense and income categories
- The ability to input due dates for monthly bills such as rent and utilities, with bill reminders
- The ability to import your bank statement by file or through automatic update through your banking website. This is great because it takes a lot of the data entry out of your budgeting.
- The ability to mark items as paid.
- The ability to go back indefinitely to see what you spent in different categories at any given previous date or month.
- Generation of complex reports so that you can see exactly where your money is going and where you are lacking in your budgeting and spending habits.

Finding the Right Software

It can be very hard to tell which software is going to be the best for you. Even with detailed lists of features and screenshots you never know what you are getting or how it works until you get in there and use it. This makes choosing a software very difficult and nerve racking.

The best way to choose a budgeting software is to sign up for free trials. You can buy software at the store, but this is not recommended. If you don't like it you're probably out the money and can't get it back. You can get the same software online, and usually with a free trial version. You can use the free trail to see how you like it, then purchase a full license when you find the right one.

The only downside to this is that not all of the features of the software may be accessible in the free trial version. You should, however, be able to see for yourself what features are available. Some software companies offer a free trial version that you can play with but can't save any data in. This way you can experiment with all of the features before spending money on the actual software.

You shouldn't buy any software without being certain it's the one you want to use. You can spend a lot of money on software that you hate before finding the right one. Make sure you will be happy with your choice. A lot of software is pretty expensive. Don't make the investment until you are ready. Getting advice and recommendations from friends and family is also a good idea. You can see the software from their computer before making a decision.

Mobile Apps

There are tons of mobile apps for budgeting. You can even get mobile apps that use the envelope method but digitally instead of actual cash in envelopes. There are mobile apps for tracking your expenses and apps for creating budgets.

The upside of using mobile apps is that you can take your budget with you wherever you go. All you need is your smart phone and you will have your budget at your fingertips. This makes it much easier to track your spending because you can enter expenses as you pay them instead of trying to remember to enter them later when you access a computer.

The downside to mobile apps is that they are severely limited. Everything has to be entered by hand. They don't have a lot of features. They are basically just a way to track your spending. You probably can't get much in the way of overviews or reports on how you are doing with your spending and budgeting. They will also have predetermined expense and income categories that cannot be customized.

Comprehensive Applications

Technology is a wonderful thing, and it is advancing quickly. There are some budgeting tools that you can use that make use of computer, web and smart phone, all wrapped into one neat, if complex, package.

Essentially these applications store all of your data in a cloud. You can access it using software on your computer, through a website, or through a smart phone app. All three are seamlessly connected as long as you have access to the internet and update each application.

In this way you enter information only one time. You have different levels of information available to you depending on which platform you are using at the time. You can have the convenience of being able to track expenses while you are on the go with the ability to use more complex features when on the computer.

Even though your information is stored on a cloud in order to make it accessible across platforms, you can save your data directly to your computer. This way if you ever stop using the service or you want to go back and look at old reports you can do so easily. You can usually save the data in a format that is easily accessible later without the software, such as in a spreadsheet format.

These applications can be much more expensive than others, although it is becoming more and more common for web apps to have an accompanying mobile app. Sometimes you will have to pay separately for the web app and sometimes it is free to people who have a paid account with the service. Either way, it may be well worth it to go this route if you are constantly on the go but need to have the more complex features offered outside of a mobile app.

Making and Implementing a Plan

Now that you are familiar with the different methods of budgeting and the tools available to you, it is time to make a plan. You need to decide which budgeting method you will use and how you will implement it. This is the most important part of your budgeting adventure.

Choosing the Method Right for You

You will need to first choose the right method for you. Should you use envelope budgeting, budget by payday, or budget by month? Here are some things to consider when making your choice.

Envelope	Payday	Month
Very few expenses	Few monthly fixed expenses	Several monthly bills
One or two sources of income	One or two sources of income	Multiple sources of income
Mostly work with cash	Combination of cash and checking account	Primarily checking account and credit cards
Fixed or variable expenses that are predictable	Fixed or variable expenses that may or may not be predictable	Fixed or variable expenses that are predictable
Varied or set income	Set or varied but predictable income	Predictable set income
Few long term goals (goals of two to three months)	Several longer term goals (goals of six months to one year)	Very long term goals (goals of one year or more)

It is possible to use a combination of methods. You may want to use both a monthly and a payday budget. You can use the monthly budget to lay out all of the bills you need to take care of for the month, then use the payday budget to distribute your money appropriately to make sure everything is covered. You might use the payday budget version but use envelopes to help you curb your spending in certain categories.

It is really all about what works for you. Choose one method or a combination of methods that makes sense to you for a start. Make sure you stick to your method of choice for at least three months to see how it works. By the end of that time you should have a good idea of whether or not it is working for you, why it is or is not working, and how you might change up your methods to make it work better.

Choosing Your Tools

Spreadsheets, basic apps and software, complex software, web apps and mobile apps—oh my! There are so many tools to choose from! Try not to go any more complex than you have to. The easier it is to budget the more likely you will be to stick to it. Keep things as automated as possible. Spreadsheets are the most complicated to set up, but among the easiest to use with the exception of having to enter all data manually.

The following table will help you determine which software, mobile app or web app tools are for you. You will want to make sure you consider your options carefully. You may want to use a combination of tools, such as a basic budgeting software with a separate mobile expense tracker.

Once you have chosen a tool you should stick with it for several months. Give it a fair chance. If you are new to budgeting you will be in unfamiliar territory no matter which tools you use. They may not seem helpful at first, but once you get used to them they could work just the way you need them to.

If you use a tool for a while and decide it is not working for you, definitely move to a different one. By that point you will have a good idea of what you need to make budgeting easiest for you.

Basic Software and Web Apps	Mobile Apps	Web Apps	Complex Software	Comprehensive Tools
One income category	One income category	Few income categories	Multiple income categories and types	Multiple income categories and types
Few and only basic expense categories	Few and only basic expense categories	Several expense categories, may not be able to create own	Many expense categories, can create your own by expense and type	Many expense categories, can create your own by expense and type
Manual entry	Manual entry	Manual entry	Import spending directly from bank website	Import spending directly from bank website and manual entry
Only accessible by computer (except web apps)	Only accessible by smart phone	Accessible from any computer with internet, not usually compatible with mobile phones	Accessible only from your primary computer where the software is installed	Accessible from computer, web or mobile phone
Input data from one location	Input data right when you spend or get money	Input data as soon as you have web access	Input data only when at your computer, could forget expenses	May be able to input data on the go, possible only from computer
Often free	Free or very inexpensive	Subscription based, usually reasonable but can add up over time	Fairly expensive but only pay one time. Get a free trial first if possible.	Very costly, may have to pay for software, subscription and mobile
Few security features	Few security features, but little personal information included	All information stored in a cloud with good security, but is web based so caution needed	Only on your computer, secure with firewalls and protection software. Personal data stored.	Comprehensive security, but still some information via web so caution is necessary. Personal data stored.

Making Goals and Sticking to Them

All of your best intentions for budgeting could go right out the window if you don't have goals. Sticking to those goals can be difficult and sometimes very challenging, but if you don't stick to them then all of your effort in budgeting will be for nothing. This is the most important step to take on your journey to financial stability.

Start Small

Start with small, very attainable goals. All goals should be measurable and timed as well. For example, don't just say that you will make it from paycheck to paycheck with all of your bills paid. Instead, make the goal that you will pay your rent on time or early for six months in a row.

If you start with a goal of saving money to buy a house, but you haven't gotten past the paycheck to paycheck mentality, you are setting yourself up for failure. You have to start with the smallest, most basic goals and work your way up from there.

After you have paid your rent on time for six months, make the goal to pay off a credit card. Pay an extra amount above the minimum balance for a few months and enjoy seeing your credit score go up.

These small steps will help prepare you for larger goals and working your way to financial stability and freedom. As you accomplish each small goal you will feel a sense of pride. You will begin to feel better about your overall financial situation and your ability to make improvements over time. Each victory, regardless of how small, is important and will eventually lead to great things.

What are your goals?

Before you can stick to your guns and accomplish your goals you need to have a clear idea of what they are. Start by making a list of several short term financial goals you want to accomplish. These might be paying bills on time, avoiding late fees, making past due utility bills current, or saving a few hundred dollars for a down payment on a car.

Next, make a list of financial goals you want to accomplish within the next year. This might be to have $50 left at the end of each pay period, or to save $100 per month in a savings account. It should still be a list of smaller, very attainable goals, but ones that might take more than a few months to accomplish.

Finally, make a list of long term goals. These are financial goals you want to attain within two to five years. This is where you dream big. Do you want to save money for a down payment on a house? Do you want to save up for your wedding? Maybe you need to give your child a good start for college. Whatever the case may be, make your big goals here. You will be surprised when you start attaining them over time.

Making a Plan

Use all of your choices in methods, tools and goals to set a definite plan for your budgeting. Know exactly what you will spend, where and when. Plan out how you will attain your short term and long term goals. Lay a solid plan.

You should write down your plan on paper or type it up on the computer. Make it very clear and concise. Plan for every contingency. When you begin feeling down, when you feel broke, when you feel as though everything is falling apart, when you feel that your budgeting is not succeeding—get out this plan and review it. This will help you stay on track or get back on track, and help you see what you are working toward. When you make progress and reach your goals in the future you can look back and see how far you've really come.

Sticking to Your Plan

It can be very hard to stick to a plan once you have it down on paper. Everything looks good on paper, but that doesn't mean it's easy to implement. Things could be pretty rocky at first. But if you stick to your budgeting it will become easier, until eventually it is second nature.

The most important thing you can do to help you stick to your plan is to create habits. Set a specific time each day that you will sit down and input all of your expenses into your budgeting tools. If you are using a mobile app, get yourself in the habit of entering expenses as soon as you pay for them.

Schedule budgeting by creating a set time each week that you will sit down and create your budget for that payday, or that month. If you don't do active budgeting every week, spend the off weeks between budgets reviewing your budget and seeing where you stand. This way you can make adjustments if necessary. Spend at least thirty minutes every week just reviewing your budget, not including time spend entering data.

The hardest thing about sticking to a budget is to curb your spending. You have to get into the habit of not spending money earmarked for other things. If you are trying to save money this can be especially difficult. Head off this bad spending by creating habits that will stop you in your tracks.

Don't carry very much cash on you. Cash is easier to spend. If you know that you don't have any money to spare after bills and groceries, don't carry your bank card on you either. Stash it in a safe place in your home where it can be accessed if needed. By not carrying your money on you, you can't spend it on a whim.

If you have credit cards and don't want to spend on them, keep one card for emergencies in your glove box and put the rest away. If you have an emergency you can get the card out of your car. If you are somewhere and want to spend money, you have to go all the way back out to the parking lot to get your card. That gives you the long walk from the register to your car and back to think about whether or not you really need that new pair of shoes.

You can also help yourself stay on track by giving yourself constant reminders of what you are working toward. Tape up pictures on your wall by your computer or put one in your wallet that represents what you are working toward. If your ultimate goal is to be able to make a better life for your family, keeping a picture of your family in your wallet will help you think twice before making unnecessary expenditures. If you are working toward buying a house, tape up a picture of the kind of house you want on the inside of your checkbook or wallet.

In the end, it is will power that will help you stick to your plan. How badly do you want to succeed? What does it really mean to you? If you are serious about your budgeting plans, you will be able to stick it out and make it work. If you falter just pick yourself back up and start again. You'll get it, and you'll reap the rewards.

Conclusion

It is a simple thing to decide that you are going to start budgeting your money to try to make your financial life better. It is quite another to put that decision into action. There are many things that go into a good budgeting journey.

By now you should have a clear understanding of what it takes to be financially responsible and stable. It is not necessarily an easy path. It is, however, a path that will lead you to everything you could want in life.

You now know about the different methods of budgeting and all of the tools you can use to help you reach your financial goals. You know how to evaluate your situation and choose the right methods and tools for you. You even know how to implement them.

The rest is up to you. Make your plan, stick to your plan, and reap the rewards. Budgeting is not just about survival. It is about making a better life.

You may be needing to budget just to get by. You may have realized that you aren't getting your bills paid on time, you're living on raman, macaroni and cheese, and hot dogs. You may realize that you have suddenly found yourself starting a family and you need to be able to provide for that family. You may simply realize you want more from life.

Where you start now with your budgeting will not be where you end up. As you start on your path you may be living paycheck to paycheck. But if you budget wisely and make good, smart goals, you will soon find yourself on an altered path. Your path will lead you to budget in new ways, to reevaluate your spending and your goals, and reach for even higher dreams.

Never underestimate the power of good budgeting. The wealthiest people in the world budget their money. They capitalize on their investments, leaving the bulk of their money alone and limiting their spending to a specified amount, spent in a specified way. Successful budgeting is the key to success for all of your financial goals, regardless of how much money you may have.

Get started on your path now, without delay. You have already made an important step in the right direction by reading this book. Take your commitment to the next level by choosing a budgeting method and one or more tools to help you on your way. You will be glad you did.

Annexes

Annex 1: Pay Period Budget

	Budget for Pay Period _____ to _____									
Income		**Budgeted**	**Actual**	**Month Expected**	**So Far**					
	Balance Forward									
	Income 1									
	Income 2									
	Income 3									
	Income 4									
								Actual	**Budgeted**	**Difference**
Total		$0.00	$0.00				**Total Income**	$0.00	$0.00	$0.00
							Total Expenses	$0.00	$0.00	$0.00
Expenses		**Budgeted**	**Actual**	**Month Expected**	**So Far**		**Difference**	$0.00	$0.00	$0.00
	Rent									
	Car Payment									
	Internet									
	Cell Phones									
	House Payment									
	KCPL									
	MGE									
	Credit Card Pays									
	Groceries									
	Work Food									
	Kids Lunch									
	Car Gas									
	Household									
	Medical									
	Dining Out									
	Clothing									
	Entertainment									
	Gifts									
	Other									
Total		$0.00	$0.00							

Annex 2: Expense Tracker

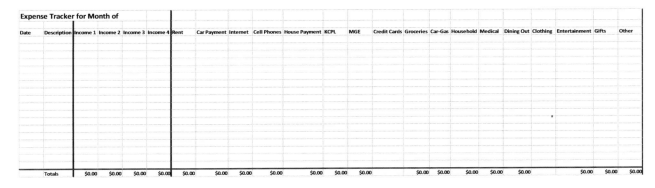

Date	Description	Income 1	Income 2	Income 3	Income 4	Rent	Car Payment	Internet	Cell Phones	House Payment	KCPL	MGE	Credit Cards	Groceries	Car-Gas	Household	Medical	Dining Out	Clothing	Entertainment	Gifts	Other
Totals		$0.00	$0.00	$0.00	$0.00	$0.00	$0.00	$0.00	$0.00	$0.00	$0.00	$0.00		$0.00	$0.00	$0.00	$0.00	$0.00		$0.00	$0.00	$0.00

Annex 3: Monthly Budget

Budget for Month of

Income		Budgeted	Actual						Actual	Budgeted	Difference
	Balance Forward										
	Income 1										
	Income 2										
	Income 3										
	Income 4										
Total		$0.00	$0.00			Total Income			$0.00	$0.00	$0.00
						Total Expenses			$0.00	$0.00	$0.00
Expenses		Budgeted	Actual			Difference			$0.00	$0.00	$0.00
	Rent										
	Car Payment										
	Internet										
	Cell Phones										
	House Payment										
	KCPL										
	MGE										
	Credit Card Pays										
	Groceries										
	Work Food										
	Kids Lunch										
	Car Gas										
	Household										
	Medical										
	Dining Out										
	Clothing										
	Entertainment										
	Gifts										
	Other										
Total		$0.00	$0.00								

INTRODUCTION

Money does make your world go round. Beg to disagree? Consider the best things in life that are supposedly free:

-A great marriage;

-Deep relationships;

-Peace of mind; and

-Giving to churches and charitable organizations.

You can't have a great marriage without money, at least enough of it. How many marriages have fallen apart because the inability to meet physical and financial needs have caused so much stress? You can't take your wife to dinner or a romantic getaway without money. You can't dress up well for your husband if you don't have money for clothes. You won't have time for your spouse if you're too busy trying to make ends meet.

You also can't have meaningful relationships with other people without money. Texting people require money. If you think connecting through Facebook is free, it isn't - you need money to buy a gadget and to avail of Internet connection. It also takes money to go out and spend quality time with friends. As with marriage, you can't really spend quality time with them if you're too preoccupied trying to make ends meet.

When you're honest with yourself, you'll agree that to a great extent, money is key to having peace of mind. It's easy to say God provides when you're not in need. But when you're neck-deep in debt and you don't have money to pay for this month's rent, you'll probably be singing a different tune.

Lastly, no matter how much you want to finance the great work your church or your favorite charitable organization is doing, you can't do that without extra money. If you aren't able to provide for your needs, how can you provide for others'?

If you're ready to start successfully managing your personal finances, turn the page and let's go!

PERSONAL FINANCE 101

"Many people take no care of their money till they come nearly to the end of it, and others do just the same with their time." – Johann Wolfgang von Goethe

Now that's a very good point to consider – taking care of money. Why should we take care of our money? Isn't money supposed to take care of us? I mean, that's why we – as Donna Summer sang – work hard for the money, right?

Yes, money is supposed to take care of us – our needs and wants. But money can't take care of itself. Like a puppet that's manipulated for the entertainment pleasure of the audience, so is money controlled for our purposes. It's something that needs to be actively controlled to enjoy the benefits. And this is where personal finance management comes in.

Personal finance management is basically the art and science of managing money in order to ensure that our needs are met. If you'd like to include wants in the definition, feel free to do so. At the core, however, personal finance management is about meeting needs so even if you're not able to meet some or most of your wants, you still managed your personal finances well.

But then again, we all want some life sweeteners now, don't we?

For purposes of personal finance management, we can classify our needs according to time: current and future. Current needs are obviously those that need to be met now and on a regular basis such as food, clothing, shelter, transportation, electricity, water and for some, medicines. Future ones include the tuition fees of our children once they are of age to study, medical and hospital expenses in the event of an unexpected medical condition that will require being confined and retirement.

Most people think they're already doing a good job of managing their personal finances because they're still alive, which means they're able to meet their needs even if it's just getting by. But if we consider the primary goal of personal finance management, which is to meet all needs, as well as the kind of needs, we'll find that meeting current needs doesn't make for successfully managing our finances. Successfully managing our finances including being able to address future needs at least to a great extent.

THE RIGHT TIME

There's a saying that haste makes waste. It may be true for many things but not potential matters of life and death. I mean, what would you think of me if I told the driver of an ambulance carrying a person who figured in serious car accident to drive slowly because haste makes waste? Right! You'd say I was nuts for applying a principle outside it's true context. It's the same with personal finances. Haste minimizes or prevents waste.

What kind of waste are we talking about here? First of all, time. Unlike wasted money, which can be earned again, wasted time is gone forever. We can't recoup the losses.

Another waste is opportunity. As David Bolyard once said: "Seize the moment for some opportunities don't come twice." What are some of these opportunities?

The first opportunity we'll miss by delaying personal finance management is a lighter savings and investment burden. What do we mean by this? When we start saving and investing earlier than later, we'll have more time to save and invest for our future needs, which means the amount of money we need to save and invest regularly is less compared to starting later. Consider 2 simple mathematical examples:

$100 ÷ 10 years = $10/year

$100 ÷ 5 years = $20/year

Do you see how our financial burden can be lessened when we have a longer time to save up and invest for future needs, which is possible when we start managing our personal finances as early as possible?

Another opportunity we can miss by delaying personal finance management is being able to successfully meet a future need. Why? One of the biggest reasons is inflation, which is the rate at which prices of our needs increase. Strictly speaking, inflation rate is a number computed by economists, which tell us how much the prices of basic commodities have gone up in the last 12 months. A published inflation rate of 5% for last month for example, means that the basic costs of living went up by 5% on average from the same month last year.

What does it have to do with missing the opportunity to provide for future needs? Say you want to have your own house by the time you retire in 10 years and that the average price of a decent home these days is $100,000.00. This means you'll have to save and invest at least $10,000 annually. But because the prices of houses, as with most other things, continue to go up every year, the money you would've saved by the time you retired in 10 years ($100,000) will no longer be enough because the average prices of decent homes by then would've gone up significantly due to inflation. When you manage your personal finances well, you get the opportunity to either have enough money to buy a decent house in by the time you retire or be able to lock in on the price of houses now even if you don't have the money yet.

Another future need – one that's sure to come up – is retirement. Consider your average monthly living expenses today and multiply it by the number of months you expect to live after retiring. The total amount you arrived at won't be the actual amount you'll need – you'll need much more because of inflation. By the time you retire, the average cost of living will be significantly higher. Personal finance management can help you take care of that.

ACCRUAL AND CASH CONCEPTS

One relatively technical thing we'll need to get a good grasp of when it comes to personal finance management is the concepts of accrual and cash method of recording financial transactions. Let's talk about the accrual method first.

Under the accrual method of recording financial transactions, income is recorded or recognized as they are earned, not when they are received. Expenses, on the other hand, are recorded as they are incurred, not when they are paid out. What does this mean in layman's terms?

Let's say you're an engineer and you earn a living as a private practitioner. After completing a project, you are now entitled to your pay as stated in your contract or agreement with your client. Under the accrual method, you already record the income now because you already earned it, i.e., you now have a valid legal claim to such money because you already completed the agreed upon service. So your income for this month would reflect the pay from this project.

Under the cash method however, you won't record it as income just yet because you haven't received the payment. If the client pays you next month, only then will you record it as income.

As for expenses, consider your monthly electric bill. When you receive your billing statement, it's usually payable on a certain date in the future. You're given a grace period from the time you're billed to the time you pay the amount. Under the accrual method, you already record it as an expense for the current period because you already have a valid legal obligation to pay the amount, even if it's in the future. Under the cash method however, you record it as an expense for the particular period wherein you actually pay for it.

So what's the big deal about the different methods? Income and expenses will be recorded either way so why do we need to be aware of both? The reason: liquidity.

Liqui-what? Liquidity refers to our ability to meet our financial obligations as they fall due. Personal finance is about liquidity because we need money, not claims to money, to pay for our needs and wants. Let me illustrate.

For simplicity's sake, let's assume you only have one source of income – consultancy services – and only one expense – apartment rental. Further, let's assume you earned $1,500 from being a company's consultant but the terms of conditions of that engagement state that you'll be paid on the 2nd Monday of the following month. The rental on your apartment, however, is due at the end of the current month. Even if your income is 2 times your monthly rental, it won't mean much if you don't get it on time in order to pay the rent.

The risk with using the accrual method for recording and planning is that it doesn't take into consideration the timing of receipt and spending of cash. Using the accrual method for the above-mentioned example, you may think you're doing well because income significantly exceeds expense for the month but it doesn't tell you that you don't have the money to pay for the expense during the period. The cash method of recording and planning allows you to minimize your liquidity risk or the risk that you won't be able to meet your financial obligations. You'll appreciate this concept better in Chapter 2 on cash flow management.

TIME VALUE OF MONEY

One of the cornerstones of personal finance management is the concept of the time value of money, which states that our money that's available now is worth more than the same amount in the future because of the opportunity to make it grow. To put it another way, we'd be better off receiving, say, $100 now instead of $100 a year from now because we have the opportunity to make the money grow between now and 12 months later. This is the reason for charging interest on borrowed money and earning money from investments, particularly from lending money. This concept is the foundation for investing as well as debts.

OVERVIEW

The rest of this book will be dedicated to helping you meet your current and future needs by teaching you how to manage your finances properly through cash flow management (including budgeting), debt management, saving and investing your savings well. I will explain these concepts to you in a simple and straightforward manner so that you'll be able to really grasp these key concepts and help you understand more advanced personal finance reading materials later on.

CASH FLOW MANAGEMENT

"The fact is that one of the earliest lessons I learned in business was that balance sheets and income statements are fiction. Cash flow is reality." – Chris Chocola

Money moves in 2 ways: into our accounts or wallets and away from them. These movements are called cash flows and when it comes to ensuring our current and future needs are met, this is the key that'll spell success or failure in terms of personal finance management.

Why is that so? Remember liquidity or the ability to meet financial obligations when they fall due? It's dependent on how much cash we have and that is dependent on how we manage our cash flows. When we allow more money to move away from us compared to what moves into our accounts and wallets, our liquidity is compromised.

INFLOWS, OUTFLOWS AND POSITIONS

Events that move cash into our accounts and wallets are called cash inflows while those that move cash out from our accounts and wallets are called cash outflows. Examples of cash inflows are salaries, cash gifts and cash prizes won. Examples of cash outflows include bills payment, donating to a charitable institution, buying clothes or giving tithes and offerings in church.

If our cash inflows exceed outflows during a certain period, we experience what is called a positive cash flow position. When cash outflows exceed cash inflows, we are in a negative cash flow position. When both are equal, we have a square or neutral position.

Neutral positions mean that we are only able to meet current needs and without any surplus or savings, we won't be able to set anything aside for future needs. It also increases our liquidity risk – the possibility that we won't be able to meet our financial obligations – because if something happens to us that'll negatively affect our cash inflows, we don't have any savings or buffer to cover cash outflows.

Negative cash positions obviously mean we aren't able to meet current needs at all. Aside from failing to meet our current needs, being in a consistent state of negative cash flows every month will bury us deep in bad debts, which we'll discuss further in Chapter 3. Suffice to say, this can become a downward spiral of increasing bad debts and eventually, bankruptcy.

The ideal cash position is a positive one, which means we're not just able to meet current needs but we're also able to put aside money to provide for future ones. Unfortunately, consistent positive cash flows aren't easy to do because human nature gravitates toward spending as much money as is available. Enjoying positive cash flows may require a great deal of discipline and consistency to achieve but it's well worth it.

MAXIMIZING CASH INFLOWS

To maximize cash inflows, we need to identify 2 sources: recurring and non-recurring. Recurring sources – those that regularly provide cash inflows – include your job, business, certain types of investments and for some people, allowances from parents or companies. These sources are crucial to meeting our current needs because they offer a great degree of stability and consistency. Because current needs are recurring, most of our cash inflows should also be from recurring sources.

Non-recurring sources include work bonuses that are contingent on our personal and the company's performance, cash gifts, proceeds of sales of personal assets and occasional side income. We shouldn't rely on these for current needs because as we said, stability and consistency is key to meeting such needs and these neither stable nor consistent. These are good for complementing recurring sources, especially for saving up and investing for future needs.

One key to maximizing cash inflows is by establishing as many sources of recurring income as possible, also known by a more technical term called diversification. Basically, we don't want to put all our eggs in one basket, just in case that basket falls. By having several sources of recurring cash inflows, we lower the risk for disrupted cash inflows.

Another key to maximizing cash inflows is to establish recurring sources that are passive. Passive recurring income sources are those that require minimal active involvement in order to generate cash. In other words, these are sources that you can pretty much leave alone to produce cash inflows. Because these sources don't require much of your time and attention, you can set up more recurring sources of cash inflows and thus maximize them. We'll talk more about passive sources of recurring income – also known as passive investments – in Chapter 5.

[Excerpt from the first 3 Chapters – for complete book, please purchase on Amazon.com]

59657627R00024

Made in the USA
San Bernardino, CA
06 December 2017